BADASS BLACK MEN AFFIRMATIONS

DAILY POSITIVE THOUGHTS TO INCREASE
CONFIDENCE, CREATE WEALTH, ATTRACT SUCCESS,
AND BOOST SELF-ESTEEM FOR THE POWERFUL
BLACK MAN

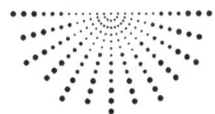

PRESTON GREENE
JASMINE GREENE

CONTENTS

To my wife, who has shown me all that I have to offer to the world and encouraged me to inspire others.

INTRODUCTION

When my wife started listening to affirmations and making them part of her everyday routine, it felt too good to be true. I remember thinking to myself, "So all I have to do is listen and repeat affirmations out loud and my wildest dreams will come true... yeah, right!"

As a man, when I thought about achieving all my dreams and goals, affirmations were not on the list. I thought about the "hustle"! I believed that I would make my dreams come true because I had the discipline to wake up at 5 a.m., the determination to push through adversity, and the skills to go above and beyond. Years later, I still dreaded waking up every morning, counted down the days till the weekend, had a horrible self-image, and held on to hate and resentment.

It took me a long time to realize that what I feed my mind with significantly influenced my attitude and decisions. It didn't matter what actions I took if I had a poor mindset through it all.

I eventually put aside my ego and added affirmations to my daily morning routine. I became my own cheerleader and reminded myself every day that I was loved, supported, and had the potential to do anything.

This is my success story, and yours starts today. Use this book to remind yourself that you deserve the life you want. Affirmations are not some woo-woo activity only for women, but instead have the potential to change your life if used correctly.

All the affirmations in the following chapter are designed to empower, encourage, and support you on your journey. There is no right or wrong way to read these affirmations. You can go through chronologically or jump ahead to a chapter you are struggling with. Each chapter is designed to provide you with confidence and abundance in that area of your life.

To get the most out of this book, you can read the affirmations in your head or out loud. Take the necessary time to say each saying with conviction and the belief that this is the new you.

As you navigate through challenges, keep this book handy as a constant reminder that you're here for a purpose and you deserve to fulfill all your dreams.

START YOUR DAY OFF RIGHT

1. Today I am filled with happiness and joy.

2. I will live today trying to impress only myself.

3. Today I will love myself first and then do everything else.

4. I am going to have a great day because only my attitude determines my stress levels.

5. I will be productive today.

6. I remain calm in chaotic situations.

7. I am going to push away toxic people today.

8. I am not going to indulge in negative thoughts today.

9. One bad moment will not define my day.

10. I will conquer all of my goals for the day.

11. I am going to have a positive approach towards life today.

12. I can and will dictate how my day will go.

13. Today I will be happy.

14. I am going to work a little harder than yesterday.

15. I will not stress unnecessarily today.

16. No matter what challenges I face, I am going to face them like a man.

17. I will always focus on the positive today.

18. I am going to complete all my tasks on my to-do list today.

19. I will approach today with a sense of confidence.

20. I am better today than I was yesterday.

21. I am going to succeed today, even if they are just small successes.

22. Today it is okay not to be perfect and so is tomorrow.

23. I'm alive and capable of anything today.

24. Today, I will do my best in everything that I do.

25. I will show gratitude when I'm thankful.

26. I will have fun and laugh through each and every day.

27. I am going to have a good day.

2

BUILD THE SELF-ESTEEM OF AN ALPHA MALE

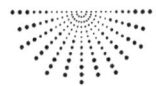

1. I am respected and loved by others.

2. Others see me as powerful and self-assured.

3. I would be happy to be born again as a black man.

4. Confidence is my birthright.

5. I am proud of who I am.

6. I will always hold my head high.

7. I have confident body language.

8. I am a strong black man who deserves all the good things in life.

9. I have learned that the true definition of respect will only appear if I decide to respect myself.

10. I am proud of my upbringing.

11. Instead of impressing others, I like to impress myself.

12. I am more than just a somebody.

13. I believe in myself.

14. The only responsibility I have is to myself.

15. I am proud of how far I've come.

16. I live my life to please myself and nobody else.

17. I am proud of the man I continue to become.

18. I am content with myself no matter what others think of me.

19. My posture is confident.

20. I am an honorable man first and foremost.

21. I will not judge myself and neither should anyone else.

22. I am proud of myself.

23. Self-confidence is what I thrive on.

24. I am filled with love for myself.

25. My color is my strength.

26. I have a powerful, masculine presence.

27. I will respect myself even when others don't.

28. I am comfortable in any situation.

29. My kindness and empathy make me a better human.

30. I am comfortable with my own skin.

31. My black skin is magnificent.

32. I am important because I define my own self-worth and nobody else.

33. My confidence does not stem from the compliments of others.

34. People admire my strength of character and compliment me on my self-confidence.

35. I am proud of my culture.

36. I matter. My beliefs matter. My voice matters.

37. People love me for who I am.

38. I matter to this world.

39. I am beautiful inside and out.

40. I see the mirror and I love it.

41. My color has made me unique.

42. I am happy with myself.

43. I accept myself for who I am.

44. I am proud of the person that I am becoming.

45. I am black and strong.

46. I will not compare myself to others.

47. My confidence comes from competence.

48. I love myself.

49. I am worthy, just like every human.

50. I am happy to be born as a black man.

51. I am an alpha male.

52. I understand that I am a work-in-progress with a ton of potential.

53. I am happy in my own skin.

54. I am black and proud.

ATTRACT YOUR DREAM CAREER

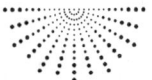

1. I am talented enough to do whatever I want.

2. I will find my niche.

3. My efforts are commendable.

4. I believe in my dreams and my ability to achieve them.

5. I have a great relationship with my boss and my co-workers.

6. I can succeed at whatever I choose.

7. I will never shy away from any guidance.

8. I love my career path.

9. My opinions and ideas are respected and valued.

10. I deserve success.

11. I am assertive, passionate and intense.

12. I am a leader.

13. I am good at my job, and I love what I do.

14. I work hard in my life and I deserve to be happy.

15. I am a valuable asset to my team.

16. I will never lessen my standards for anyone.

17. I am performing well in my career and will continue to learn how to do even better.

18. My opinion and ideas are valuable.

19. I am in control of everything that I do.

20. I will look inward to find my true purpose in life.

21. I can get any job I want.

22. I am rising slowly but steadily.

23. I have a vision and I work for it.

24. I am highly respected.

25. I am an asset, not a liability.

26. I can be an expert in any field.

27. I am innovative and tenacious.

28. I have great ideas.

29. My job provides the opportunity to work towards my financial goals.

30. Nobody else can do my job as well as me.

31. My mind has creative ideas and they deserve to be heard.

32. I am giving my best and expect the best from my career.

33. I am knowledgeable enough to do this.

34. I am a creative and influential thinker.

4
BUILD FINANCIAL ABUNDANCE

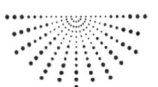

1. I let go of all my fears around money.

2. If others can be wealthy, so can I.

3. I constantly discover new sources of income.

4. There are countless opportunities to make more money in my life.

5. I can leverage my skills to bring in more money at any time.

6. My income is growing higher and higher.

7. My income will exceed my expenses.

8. I am so excited about receiving more money.

9. Money flows to me freely as I move through this world.

10. I am what a wealthy person looks like.

11. I accept abundance.

13. I embrace new avenues of income.

14. Manifesting money is easy because I'm ready to put in the work.

15. I am financially free.

16. I am an amazing good luck generator.

17. My mind is a powerful magnet for wealth and abundance.

18. I am not poor; I am on the path to a wealthy life.

19. Financial freedom is not just a dream; it will be my reality.

20. The more fun I have, the more money I make.

21. I am so happy and grateful that money flows to me easily and effortlessly.

22. My bank account is constantly filled with money.

23. I always have enough money.

24. There is no limit to the amount of money I am capable of earning.

25. I deserve to be rich.

5
OVERCOME FAILURE, FEAR, AND ANXIETY

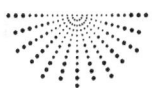

1. I choose to always react positively to all situations.

2. I'm safe and under no threats from the world.

3. Humility is at the heart of learning from my mistakes.

4. As I relax and slow my breathing, anxiety flows out.

5. I know that my own success and failure are in my hands.

6. I deserve good things in life.

7. It's perfectly okay to smile when I'm happy and cry when I'm sad.

8. I am not afraid of my truth anymore.

9. I choose to forgive myself and release myself from the past.

10. I am not afraid of change.

11. There is a positive perspective to every situation.

12. My choices matter in so many ways and I believe I am making the right ones.

13. I will never give up.

14. My mistakes are stepping stones for success.

15. With every breath I take, I choose to inhale the good and exhale the bad.

16. I am liberated from the fear of failure.

17. I am bigger than my circumstances.

18. I know that I am a brave and strong individual. Therefore, I know that I will be okay.

19. I will continue to get stronger day by day.

20. I breathe in confidence and breathe out all fear.

21. The situation isn't good or bad.

22. I speak my mind without fear of rejection.

23. My mistakes were nothing more or less than mistakes and I have learned from them.

24. Fear no longer has any advantage over me.

25. I am deciding to feel calm and think positive, nurturing thoughts.

26. I choose to live my life with an open heart.

27. I hear black and I think of power and strength.

28. I am strong.

29. I take risks even when I feel fear.

30. There's no obstacle that I can't overcome.

31. My failures made me the amazing person I am today.

32. Giving up is not an option for me.

33. My past experiences can't stop me from succeeding in future

34. I am doing my best.

35. I inhale confidence and exhale doubts.

36. Uncertainty makes me stronger.

37. I am not sacred of tough situations.

38. I am fearless.

6

REMEMBER TO SAY "THANK YOU"

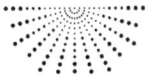

1. I am so blessed for everything I have.

2. I am grateful for everything the Universe has blessed me with.

3. I am thankful to my ancestors.

4. I realize how fortunate I am that so many people love me.

5. Gratitude in challenging times helps me grow.

6. Each day blesses me with more things to be grateful for.

7. I am grateful to have the power to make my dreams come true.

8. I am thankful for my safe and secure home.

9. I am grateful for the wisdom of everyone I meet.

10. I recognize the opportunities the universe presents, and I give thanks for each one.

11. I am grateful for the constant flow of money through my life.

12. I appreciate all the things my wonderful body allows me to do.

13. I am so grateful to be alive.

14. I appreciate my strength and resilience.

15. I am so grateful for all the love in my life – given and received.

16. I live my life with awareness and gratitude.

17. I see abundance all around me, and I feel so blessed.

18. I am grateful for everything I have in my life.

19. I realize the gift of this precious human life.

20. I have access to nourishing food and clean water, and I am so thankful.

21. I am grateful for this day and another chance to improve myself.

22. I am thankful for the Universe and all her abundance.

23. I see and appreciate the light in everyone, including myself.

24. I am thankful for the ability to learn, develop, and grow.

25. Life gives me abundant blessings to be grateful for.

26. My friends enrich my life beyond measure; I am so thankful for each and every one.

27. I am grateful to the Universe for manifesting all the wonderful things in my life so far.

28. I recognize every blessing, no matter how small.

29. Each day is an opportunity and a gift.

30. I love and appreciate my beautiful family.

31. I choose to be thankful no matter my circumstances.

32. I am grateful for the abundance that I have and the abundance that's on its way.

33. I am grateful for the positive things in my life.

34. I find gratitude in every experience.

35. I gratefully receive the lessons that each experience brings.

36. I am thankful for my mistakes because they have made me stronger.

37. I find gratitude and joy every day.

38. I give thanks for each exquisite moment.

39. With a sense of gratitude, I see the world in a new light.

40. I am blessed.

41. God has given me everything.

7

STAY MOTIVATED & SMASH YOUR GOALS

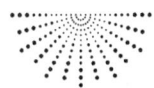

1. I am never giving up on my dreams.

2. I am heading in the right direction with my life.

3. If I find a way to change my thoughts, I know that I can change my actions.

4. I always find a way to succeed.

5. I am a work in progress, and I understand that my progress never ends.

6. I have a clear goal for my life.

7. I am free to choose the life I want.

8. Life has chosen me to flourish.

9. My potential to succeed is infinite.

10. I am a positive person.

11. I boldly go after what I want.

12. I am in control of my future and my destiny.

13. I never settle for anything but the best.

14. I take action now.

15. I am bright and intelligent.

16. I have everything that I need already within me.

17. My definition of success is my own.

18. Success attracts itself to me.

19. I am confident, strong, and powerful.

20. I bravely strive for what I want in my life.

21. I can have any lifestyle I want.

22. I am disciplined.

23. My success and failure are in my hands.

24. I can create my own path.

25. Instead of going for the least, I will always go for the most.

26. I am confident about my future.

27. I won't give up, but I will grow up.

28. I am a magnet of success.

29. I can build my own future.

30. I am successful and everyone knows it.

31. I am the hero of my own story.

32. I am courageous.

33. I am working every day to improve myself.

34. I am here to live my life the way I want to live it.

35. I define my own success; nobody else does.

36. I have everything that I desire.

37. I work hard to achieve my goal.

38. I am focused.

39. I was born as a supreme being.

40. I can always do better. I can always do more.

41. I deserve better.

42. I have a strong willpower to accomplish my dreams.

43. I am a king.

8

IMPROVE RELATIONSHIPS

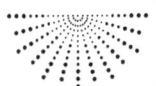

1. I deserve to be loved.

2. I give and receive love.

3. I am a king in the eyes of my family members.

4. I respect everything and everyone in my life.

5. My sensitivity as a man is important and helps me act out of love.

6. I will nurture and care for my loved ones.

7. My neighbors and community believe in me.

8. I contribute to my family's happiness.

9. I am a light to my brothers and sisters.

10. I make others feel safe and secure.

11. People are attracted to me instantly.

12. Anybody will be lucky to have me.

13. I bring out the best in people.

14. I am fun to be with.

15. People are attracted to my positive energy.

16. I make people feel valued.

17. I am a good person.

18. I deserve to be respected.

19. People around me encourage me.

20. I will not let anyone take me for granted.

21. I am an inspiration to others.

22. I will not let anyone hurt me.

23. I deserve to be happy and have a good life.

24. I am worthy of love.

25. People around me are supportive.

26. I accept a healthy relationship with everyone.

27. I accept honesty.

28. I am an asset to my community.

9

BETTER HEALTH & FITNESS

1. I am a friend to my body.

2. I accept a healthy body.

3. I forgive my body and treat it with the same loving kindness I would like to receive.

4. My body is strong.

5. I will create a healthy lifestyle for myself.

6. I will value my health as much as I value my career.

7. I love the parts of me that need the most love right now.

8. I am open to new ways of improving my health.

9. My body has done and will continue to do amazing things.

10. I am doing everything I can to help my body be well as quickly as possible.

11. I am healthy and strong.

12. My body is a gift and I love it.

13. I accept a healthy mind.

14. I allow the intelligence of my body to move my health forward.

15. Today, I have my physical health and that is enough for me.

16. My body is in the best shape/size it needs to be at this moment.

17. My health matters.

18. I feel comfortable in my skin.

19. I am worthy of good health.

20. I will always choose to prioritize my own overall health.

21. My black skin is beautiful.

22. My body knows how to heal itself.

23. I feed my Spirit. I train my body. I focus my mind. It's my time.

10

INFLUENCE & CHANGE THE WORLD

1. I am becoming an inspiring black man.

2. I will win the world with love.

3. The insignificant actions of others do not have to impact my life in a significant way.

4. My voice is dominant.

5. I am bigger than social pressure.

6. I am free from all the negativity around me.

7. I have decided to stick with love.

8. I will not let others push me around.

9. I am a product of peace and righteousness.

10. I am a healer to my family and the world.

11. Others respect me.

12. My charming energy is seen by others and helps show them why positivity matters.

13. Whether I look at the big or small picture, I can still see how important I am.

14. I was born as a leader and thinker.

15. My thoughts can change the world.

16. We are all different and it's alright.

17. I respect every human being.

18. I enjoy being the leader in social situations.

19. I have ideas that can change the world and I deserve to be heard.

20. I know that I have abilities that nobody else has and I will use them to make the world a better place.

21. I choose love over hate every day.

22. I am not a random person, I am here for a specific reason.

23. Others look to me as a leader.

24. Unity is our greatest strength.

25. My voice matters.

26. If I change my thoughts, I can change the whole world.

27. I will always do what is right.

28. My ideas are changing the world but only when I share them with others.

29. I believe in me, you and us.

11
WIND DOWN & RELAX

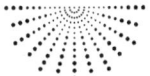

1. Life is beautiful.

2. I trust my intuition and listen to my inner voice.

3. There is more than one way to define happiness and I am not here to please anybody except myself.

4. I am living the way I want to live my life.

5. I can make myself and other people happy.

6. I am committed to the kind of life I envision.

7. I love my life.

8. I am blessed to have another beautiful day ahead of me.

9. I can and will create my own destiny.

10. My opportunities in life are endless.

11. I am right where I need to be and I do not need to live my life to please anybody else.

12. Today, I did my best. And tomorrow is another day.

13. I accept joy every day.

14. Everything that is happening now is happening for my ultimate good.

15. I am better than I was yesterday.

16. Happiness, laughter, peace, and wealth surround me because I am worthy of it.

17. I am thankful for the people I encountered today.

18. I attract miracles into my life.

19. I am in touch with my higher consciousness.

20. I will always remember to celebrate small wins.

21. I am proud to be a black man.

22. My life is full of unexpected miracles.

23. I am safe and secure with myself.

24. I know how to relax and have a good time.

25. Every day is important, either as a memory or as a lesson.

26. I release today.

CONCLUSION

Congratulations on taking the time to better yourself. Continue referencing these affirmations whenever negative thoughts or self-doubt creep in. There is never a finish line with self-improvement, and it needs to be practiced every day to see long-lasting success.

If you feel like this book helped you, it would be fantastic if you could leave a review on Amazon. Reviews will help this book reach other black men that need to be reminded of their true self-worth and power. I would also like to encourage you to share these affirmations with other black men. We are all subjected to different forms of negativity and challenges and together, we can support and encourage one another.

If you enjoyed this book and would like the audio version, you can search "365 Badass Black Men Affirmations" on Audible. Listening to affirmations can be a great way to get these statements into your subconscious mind and can easily be incorporated into life while you're driving, exercising, or getting ready for bed.

BONUS #1: AFFIRMATIONS I TELL MY CHILDREN

A lot of parents have reached out to me, wondering if affirmations could help their children. Although it's not always realistic to ask your son or daughter to listen along and repeat affirmations with you, they can be extremely beneficial for creating a positive identity from a young age.

When my son turned one, I took the time every day to give him affirmations. Anytime I was changing him or bathing him, I wanted to make sure I was filling his mind with positive, encouraging thoughts. I realized that although I couldn't change how people viewed him, I could shape how he would view the world and himself. I have continued to give him affirmations every day as he gets older, and try to frame them in response to any struggles he is going through. All of the affirmations below will help build positive self-esteem and an optimistic outlook on the world.

1. You are loved.

2. You should do what makes you happy.

3. You come from a long, rich Black heritage.

4. I trust that you will make the right decisions.

5. Your brown skin is beautiful, and it even absorbs sunlight!

6. You are special.

7. You are your only limit.

8. Your opinion matters, I'd love to hear it.

9. You get better every day.

10. There is nobody in the whole world like you.

11. Your mind is full of knowledge.

12. You are powerful

13. I love how confident you are.

14. Happiness flows through you.

15. Your skin is like a shield, it protects the amazing things you have inside from the mean things people say.

16. You have people who care for and look out for you.

17. You are destined for greatness.

18. Your imperfections are what make you perfect.

19. You are creative.

20. I believe in you.

21. You are capable.

22. Your voice is powerful.

23. Thank you for expressing your feelings to me.

24. You are a leader.

25. I accept you for who you are.

26. You can always stand up for yourself.

27. Your attitude is full of gratitude.

28. Before you were born, you were dreamed of and hoped for.

29. You can do anything you set your mind to.

30. I am so proud of who you are.

31. You are a problem solver.

32. It is okay to feel that way.

33. You are so thoughtful.

34. You can't control what people think of you, but you can show them who you are.

35. You are worthy.

36. It's okay if you don't know, this means you can learn something new.

37. You are very helpful.

38. I appreciate the energy you bring to the family.

39. You deserve respect.

40. Only answer to what you want to be called.

41. You are kind.

42. There is something in this world that only you can do. That is why you are here.

43. You are valuable.

44. How people treat you is a reflection of their character and not yours.

45. You are such a hard worker.

46. I believe in you.

47. You can achieve your goals and dreams.

48. You can make a difference.

49. Thank you for putting forth your best efforts.

50. You are as good as anyone else.

51. You are beautiful inside and out.

Join me in speaking at least one affirmation to your child every day so we can build a strong and powerful next generation.

BONUS #2: AFFIRMATIONS I TELL MY WIFE

It is extremely powerful to give our loved ones affirmations every day. It is so easy for women to forget how abundant and amazing they are if they don't have someone reminding them. I have seen relationships that are on the rocks improve dramatically when couples take the time to encourage and remind each other how special they are to the world and one another. Try implementing one of the affirmations below when your wife is deflated or down.

1. I can't wait to experience the rest of my life with you.

2. I admire your integrity and I know others do too.

3. How can I make you feel more loved?

4. I can't wait till you get home from work!

5. Your arms are the only place I want to be.

6. How can I try to understand you better?

7. I feel so safe with your protection.

8. You provide so much for us.

9. You can always make me laugh. I'm so happy I have you!

10. I missed you so much today!

11. I only want you.

12. Thank you for loving me, even when I'm not that lovable.

13. Your decisions, hard work, and loving heart make me so proud to be your wife.

14. I'm praying for you today. You've got this!

15. I can't wait to tell my friends how you helped me!

16. If that's where you want to lead us, I will follow your decision.

17. I will always respect and honor you.

18. You understand me more than anyone.

19. I can't believe how lucky I am to have you.

20. You can trust me.

21. I love knowing that you want me.

22. I know we don't always see eye to eye, but it's reassuring to know we are always on the same team.

23. I am so proud of who you are.

24. I love doing projects together.

25. I love you more today than any day before.

26. I still have moments where I am speechlessly thankful for our marriage.

I hope these affirmations improve and change your life as much as they have for me.

THE END

REFERENCES

Alexanderdavis2015, V. A. P. B. (2020, May 29). *Dear Black Man: Affirmations You Might Need to Hear*. From The Script. https://fromthescript.com/2020/05/29/dear-black-man-affirmation-you-might-need-to-hear/

B. (2021a, June 23). *72 Life-Changing Positive Affirmations For Men 2022*. Coaching Online. https://www.coaching-online.org/positive-affirmations-for-men/#5_Career-Related_Positive_Affirmations_For_Men

Davenport, B. (2022, January 18). *101 Positive Affirmations For Men*. Live Bold and Bloom. https://liveboldandbloom.com/06/self-confidence/positive-affirmations-men

K. (2021b, December 31). *250+ Money Affirmations to Catapult Your Wealth*. Money for the Mamas. https://www.moneyforthemamas.com/money-affirmations/#wealth-affirmations-for-earning-money

L. (2020, August 7). *50 Positive Affirmations For Men That They Should Practice Every Day*. Thrive Global. https://thriveglobal.com/stories/50-positive-affirmations-for-men-that-they-should-practice-every-day/

Panchal, R. (2021, April 3). *151+ Positive Affirmations for Black Men - theBrandBoy.Com*. TheBrandBoy | Creative Small Business Blog with Free Resources. https://thebrandboy.com/affirmations-for-black-men/

Rotar, S. (2021, November 22). *50+ of the Best Alpha Male Affirmations - MentalStyleProject*. Mental Style Project. https://mentalstyleproject.com/alpha-male-affirmations/

Scott, S. (2020, July 10). *35 Positive Affirmations for Men to Supercharge Your Life*. Happier Human. https://www.happierhuman.com/positive-affirmations-men/